Malika Favre

Contents

Foreword	2
Women	6
Fashion	28
Travel	54
Nature	90
Patterns	112
Geometry	146
Pop & Culture	168
Society	200
Erotica	236
Acknowledgments	264

Beauty

Everything is calm and settled in Malika Favre's apartment in Barcelona. She moved here from London a few years back and the place has been filled with interesting and inspiring objects. "That's the black and white corner, with the piano," she says, pointing to the instrument she sometimes plays to relax. "Whenever I've moved, I've always ended up on the top floor somehow. The real upgrade this time is that I can see the sea through the window."

On one wall is a big, square neon light installation, made up of large and small geometric shapes. Elsewhere, ceramics, books, tropical plants and even a skate deck emblazoned with one of Malika's graphics are all carefully arranged on the shelves.

"I left Paris for London when I was in my early 20s, which was instrumental in me becoming an illustrator," she explains. "I loved the city, its energy and the vibrancy of its creative scene. London was perfect for establishing myself in the industry. I had access to international clients and met incredibly talented people, but after 10 hectic years working as an independent illustrator I realised that my priorities had changed. The intensity I once loved just became too much. I needed a better quality of life and more sunshine, so I moved to Barcelona."

"The only thing that hasn't changed is that I still work on the sofa with my Mac. I have a desk of course, I just never use it," she laughs.

Everything here has been carefully selected for its aesthetic qualities, and looking through this book, just like visiting her apartment, you can quickly see that as an artist and illustrator, Malika has been fascinated by beauty for a very long time. However, while the women, landscapes and architecture she draws are almost always beautiful in a conventional sense – pleasing, enticing, evocative – her understanding of beauty as a concept has broadened and deepened throughout her creative journey.

Malika's earliest sense of beauty came from the environment she was brought up in. Her mother was a painter, sculptor and seamstress with equally strong aesthetic sensibilities and taught Malika to draw as a child. "I can't remember not drawing. I think I started with my mum as soon as I could and never stopped after that. Even back then she was my biggest fan and my harshest critic," she laughs.

There was no television or videogames in their apartment in the suburbs of Paris, and it was always immaculately decorated to her mother's tastes. "I remember that every single object, even the dustpan in the kitchen, had something to it. I think being a stay-at-home mum it was very important for her to surround herself with beautiful things. And looking at my flat, it is equally important to me," says Malika.

"It's the effortless part that's very interesting. It doesn't matter how many hours of work were put into a piece if the end result looks like it just happened in a second."

"When I started my career as an illustrator, I focused on a sense of fashion, glamour and aesthetic beauty," she explains. "But I quickly realised that I wanted to do more than draw beautiful women."

Just like the famous fashion illustrator René Gruau was able to conjure up a beautiful dress in a few brush strokes, Malika creates stunning and sensuous women – confident and proud of their sexuality – using just a handful of perfectly refined vector shapes. Looking at her images and absorbing their meaning is effortless for the

viewer, which makes them seem beautifully simple. However, her sublime ability to reduce everything to its ideal form took years to develop.

"It's the effortless part that's very interesting," says Malika. "It doesn't matter how many hours of work were put into a piece if the end result looks like it just happened in a second. The image is just there and it's as though it's always been there. People are drawn to it because it's clear, nothing is hidden, and the emotional effect this creates is very strong. This is beauty."

"I approached illustration much like a graphic designer would, using underlying grids and geometric structures as a backbone for each composition."

The simpler the artwork, the stronger its impact, and though it's true many of Malika's images connect at an emotional level, they often tweak the intellect as well, triggering 'a smile in the mind'. Sometimes it's through the perfect shapes she creates, and the way they flow into one another. In other cases, it's the optical illusions she conjures with repeating lines and patterns.

She first explored Op Art for *Hide & Seek*, her first solo exhibition, which was held at London's Kemistry Gallery in 2012. Known at the time for her erotic alphabets and fashionable women, black and white optical patterns weren't what people really expected from her. "It gave me the opportunity to explore something new," she says. "At that point I was fascinated by urban repetition, so I decided to abstract these structures into minimal patterns, placing women as secondary protagonists to tell the story but focusing the piece on the urban landscape."

The series explored the idea of everyday beauty, inviting viewers to look at the built environment differently, to spot and appreciate beauty in the simplest things – the shadows cast by a railing, a zebra crossing or a row of balconies.

"It also allowed me to experiment with another love of mine – geometry," Malika continues. "As a teenager, I loved maths and physics and even contemplated a career in engineering before changing my mind and enrolling in graphic design school. In the early years of my career, I approached illustration much like a graphic designer would, using underlying grids and geometric structures as a backbone for each composition."

Before becoming a full-time freelance illustrator, Malika worked at Airside, one of London's leading graphic design studios from 2006 to 2011. During that time she designed her first illustrated alphabet, featuring erotically posed bunnies forming the characters, as a personal project. Based on an actual font, it was a great example of combining her graphic design background with her illustration work. She now sees it as a decisive moment in the construction of her unique visual language.

"This fascination for geometry has never left me and is still a huge influence on the work I produce today. Structuring an image is almost a game, a jigsaw that I have to solve even if the grid I use is never fully revealed to the viewer," she says.

As her illustration career took off Malika developed a growing interest in travel, taking frequent breaks by jetting off to places like Mexico, Argentina and Asia. These journeys inspired her to depict incredible landscapes and architecture, and enabled her to study how the nature of light and shadow varies from one location to the next.

"I constantly need to feed my brain with new things. My references and influences are expanding all the time and with that, so is my sense of beauty."

"When travelling you get to discover other cultures, arts and crafts, but you also get to see new colours as well," she explains. "Shadows are never grey, they are always coloured – sometimes warm, other times cold depending on the light. Each country, each city even, has a different light. And with it, your perception of people, buildings and objects changes. As an artist, travelling gives me an opportunity to really look at things, to digest the visual information and palette of a specific place and later to translate it onto paper. I constantly need to feed my brain with new things. My references and influences are expanding all the time and with that, so is my sense of beauty."

She continues: "When I started exploring travel pieces I realised how complex nature was and visualising it meant approaching my illustrations differently. I had to go into more detail and create artwork with more depth, still retaining that minimal approach. I looked at how you treat light, shadow and volume using a minimal colour palette and as few elements as possible."

Using bold but limited palettes, Malika honed her ability to generate depth through colour progressions. Her palettes have an internal logic, one that comes from observing and understanding the relationship between colours in a tonal hierarchy. "For example, yellow can exist as the shadow of white, blue as the shadow of yellow and black as the shadow of blue… it doesn't have

"I think the day I started working on *New Yorker* covers was a turning point for me because it gave me a window to express myself and my personal opinions. I'm really grateful that their art editor, Françoise Mouly, saw that potential in my work."

to be realistic but it needs to feel right to the eye," she explains. With four simple colours she's able to abstract a fully three-dimensional scene, and by fine-tuning her colour selection she dictates the mood and atmosphere of the image.

Whether working as a commercial illustrator in advertising, editorial or publishing, or as an artist creating personal pieces, this new cinematic approach to image making has expanded Malika's opportunities. With it, she's able to introduce a more sophisticated narrative and imbue her artwork with more complex meaning. At one level, her more recent artworks evoke an emotional response and please the brain with their cleverness. At another the images give her a voice.

Alongside her desire to create more cinematic imagery – albeit in her beautifully graphical style – came a much stronger focus on editorial commissions and personal pieces. Her relationship with one publication in particular has fostered this new direction in Malika's work.

"I think the day I started working on *New Yorker* covers was a turning point for me because it gave me a window to express myself and my personal opinions," she says. "I'm really grateful that their art editor, Françoise Mouly, saw that potential in my work."

One particular cover Malika did for *The New Yorker* is special to her, and was a key point in her journey as an artist. In 2016, she was asked to send ideas for a double issue about health, medicine and the body. This took her back to an experience she had as a child. At the age of six, she had an operation to correct strabismus, a condition she was born with that caused both her eyes to wander.

"I clearly remember that short moment just before falling asleep on the operating table. It was both scary and exciting. Being a little girl with that condition wasn't always easy, especially on a social level, and I couldn't wait to have the operation and start a new life," says Malika.

Malika's surgeon was a woman and so for her *New Yorker* cover she depicted four female surgeons looking down at the viewer. "Anybody who has been under full anaesthesia can relate to that decisive moment before losing consciousness and while my experience was very personal, the image I sent to *The New Yorker* felt quite universal," she says. A few days after publication, the cover had taken on a life of its own thanks to Susan Pitt, an endocrinologist at the University of Wisconsin. Along with three other women, she decided to post an image replicating the illustration and called on all female surgeons to do the same. An online movement was born and soon thousands of pictures of women doctors were spreading all over social media.

"My illustration had become a way for women surgeons out there in a male-dominated profession to stand up and be visible. It was a very proud moment and also a real turning point for me. It made me realise how powerful my work could be," says Malika.

"To me, an image becomes more powerful when it's not only beautiful but says something important. I believe in social responsibility and I feel we have a role to play here."

Today, while she's reluctant to ride into political battles on a white horse, she favours commissions that give her room to explore things that are personal to her such as the empowerment of women, gender equality, sexuality and tolerance. Doing more issue and narrative-based projects has also led her to reassess the role beauty plays in her work.

"Creating a beautiful piece can be a very efficient way to reach more people but that concept of beauty can feel a bit vacuous at times," she says. "To me, an image becomes more powerful when it's not only beautiful but says something important. I believe in social responsibility and I feel we have a role to play here. As illustrators of the digital era, we now have a direct connection to people through social media. What we draw is seen, shared, emulated, praised or criticised, and can have a deep impact on society."

Garrick Webster

My fascination with the female form started at a very young age and as soon as I could hold a pencil I was drawing women. At first it was princesses and fairies, soon it turned into fashionistas, and later they became mature and sophisticated women.

Growing up in Paris, there was a real sense of elegance to the women walking down the street and their red lips, high heels and beautiful garments made a big impression on me and appeared heavily in my early work.

When I became an independent illustrator, women were central to my signature style. Back then, I used very few shapes and played with negative space to get to the essence of femininity. I wanted my characters to feel universal and almost anonymous by focusing all my energy on a few strokes and details to convey the overall form. This led to commissions from clients in fashion and beauty as well as editorial pieces for magazines such as *Vogue* and *Elle*.

As my interests evolved, so did my style. I started approaching female characters in more detail, bringing in shadow and volume, and in doing so infused the women I drew with more life and personality. Suddenly, it wasn't about paring down conventional beauty, it was about telling a story. Today I look at this eclectic collection of women as an expression of my own relationship to femininity – they are strong, independent, sensual and free.

Women

Moyen Format, *Afar*
Editorial illustration, 2012

Plongeoir, *Fabric*
Editorial cover, 2013

Page Turner, *The New Yorker*
Editorial cover, 2016

In the Shade, *The New Yorker*
Editorial cover, 2016

Door, *Hide&Seek Series*
Personal work, 2012

Hands, *Hide&Seek Series*
Personal work, 2012

Bohemian Girl 1, *Westbury Hotel*
Bespoke print, 2015

Bohemian Girl 2, *Westbury Hotel*
Bespoke print, 2015

Red Sparrow, *The New Yorker*
Editorial illustration, 2018

Yearbook, *Magneto*
Editorial illustration, 2019

Capeline, *Sephora*
Outdoor advertising, 2015

Tokyo, *SHOP Travel Guide*
Editorial cover, 2012

La Mercè
Festival poster, 2021

BAM, *La Mercè*
Festival poster, 2021

(Next Page)
Antimasclista, *La Mercè*
Festival poster, 2021

MAC, *La Mercè*
Festival poster, 2021

La Cursa, *La Mercè*
Festival poster, 2021

La Havana, *La Mercè*
Festival poster, 2021

Bacci di Dama, *Carluccio's*
Promotional poster, 2015

Petits Plaisirs, *Metropolitan*
Editorial cover, 2018

Stockholm, *SHOP Travel Guide*
Editorial cover, 2012

Helsinki, *SHOP Travel Guide*
Editorial cover, 2013

I have always had a fascination for fashion, especially couture pieces from designers such as Dior, Valentino and Balmain. I started doing fashion illustration early in my career for women's magazines but rapidly moved onto other themes. As much as I loved drawing dresses, I didn't want to be limited to this type of commission. Once in a while, my love for fashion would come back, in the shape of a pattern, a hat or a simple jewellery detail. I rekindled my love for garments when designing a handful of *The New Yorker* spring and fall style issues and realised that my approach to fashion had deepened without even realising it. Somehow, all the work I had developed containing optical illusions, volumes and movement came rushing back and helped me find a new way to bring these garments to life.

Fashion

Collection 9, *Louisa Parris*
Illustrations for a fashion collection, 2021

Collection 9, *Louisa Parris*
Illustrations for a fashion collection, 2021

Collection 9, *Louisa Parris*
Illustrations for a fashion collection, 2021

Composed, *The New Yorker*
Editorial cover, 2021

Sweeping into Fall, *The New Yorker*
Editorial cover, 2019

Il cappello (triptych), *Affiches*
Screen print series, 2021

Stripes
Personal work, 2011

Pin-up
Personal work, 2012

Searching for Martin Margiela, *Metropolitan*
Editorial illustrations, 2018

Dame du Soir
Personal work, 2017

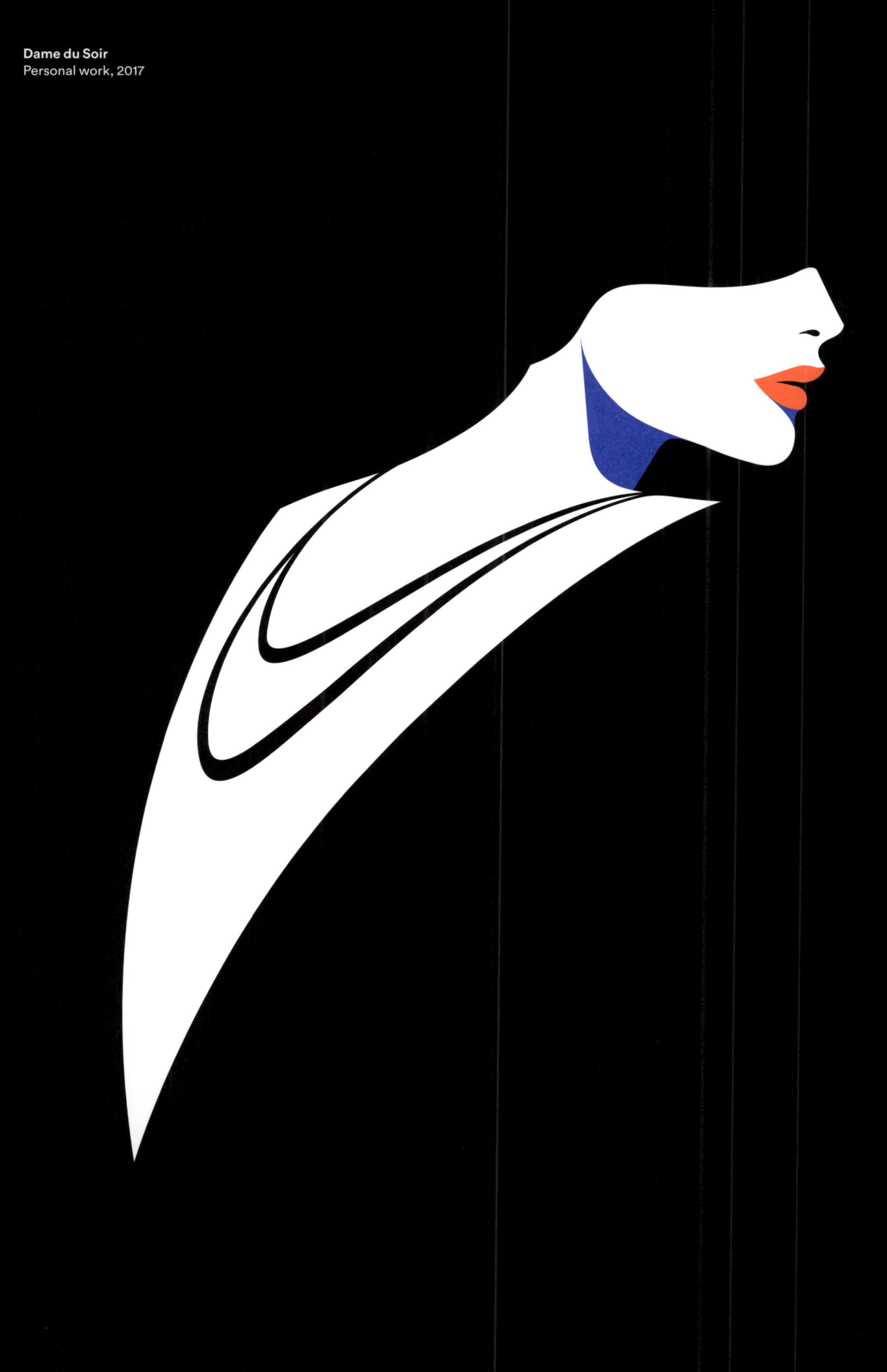

La Promenade
Personal work, 2011

How to be More French, *Stylist UK*
Editorial cover, 2016

Le Boudoir, *Vanity Fair Collection*
Editorial cover, 2016

Navy is the New Black, *The Guardian*
Editorial illustration, 2013

Fashion 50

Berlin, *Weltkunst*
Editorial cover, 2020

Spring to Mind, *The New Yorker*
Editorial cover, 2019

La Scala, *Milan Fashion Week*
Editorial cover, 2017

Hamburg, *SHOP Travel Guide*
Editorial cover, 2012

Travel is essential to my creative process and an important part of my life.

I didn't really travel much as a child, at least not to exotic destinations. My first trip was to Mexico when I was 26. Everything was new and different — the colours, the smells, the people — and I fell in love not only with the country but with the feeling itself. I came back with a head full of colours.

As soon as I became a freelance illustrator, I started travelling heavily, often working from the remote places I visited.

I took any opportunity to see a new country — from residency projects and conferences to simply joining a friend on a road trip. In a matter of years I had been to Martinique, Argentina, India, Peru and New Zealand, amongst other places.

Naturally, my expeditions made their way into my work. The first pieces I drew were inspired by the feeling of travelling itself — idealised and imaginary representations of the places I had visited. Living in London also had a lot to do with my urge to draw sunny and exotic settings. It was a way to escape reality for a day.

What fascinates me the most when discovering a new place is understanding its light. It somehow shapes your surroundings, the colours you are seeing, the taste of the food you are eating and the mood of the people you are meeting. Light is what makes a location unique, so when it comes to translating it into an image, I use it as the starting point, trying to extract a palette that conveys the feeling of the place.

My travel pieces usually result from an organic mix of experiences, photographs and memories, neither totally real nor entirely imaginary. No amount of online research will ever compete with standing in the place you want to draw, digesting all that sensorial and visual information for yourself.

Travel

On the Draw, *Canary Islands Tourism Board*
Fuerteventura exhibition series, 2014

Cliffs, *Berenberg Equity Highlights*
Editorial cover, 2017

La Côte, *Kuoni Travel*
Editorial illustration, 2017

Archipelago, *Kuoni Travel*
Editorial illustration, 2017

Les Quais, *The Parisianer*
Editorial cover, 2014

Il Était une Fois l'Orient Express, *Institut du Monde Arabe*
Exhibition poster, 2014

Cata, *Siempre Playa Project*
Promotional poster, 2018

The Red Wall, *LeBlanc*
Collaborative illustration series with Sebastian Weiss, 2020

Rendez-vous, *Domain West Hollywood*
Outdoor advertising, 2015

73 Travel

De La Warr, *Rob & Jess*
Private commission, 2016

Migration, *Geschichte*
Editorial Illustration, 2020

Croisière
Private commission, 2014

June
Personal work, 2014

Régate, *Sport&Style*
Editorial illustration, 2016

American Fliers, *The Washington Post*
Editorial illustration, 2014

Ipanema, *How Beautiful it is*
Exhibition contribution, 2014

Sortie en Mer, *WeTransfer*
Online wallpaper, 2016

6 O'clock, *Financial Times*
Editorial cover, 2015

Global Cities, *Knight Frank*
Annual report cover, 2016

Route 78, *Transport for London*
Bespoke print, 2015

Bologna, *Carluccio's*
Christmas invitation, 2013

Morning Dip
Personal work, 2017

Studio Dreams, *Nobrow*
Book contribution, 2018

Nature is a theme I started exploring recently and that somehow always takes me back to my art school years in Paris. I remember drawing plants and birds for hours and if I am being honest, feeling incredibly bored by it. Back then all I was interested in was the human form. But I strongly believe that practice helped me tremendously when I finally started adding flora and fauna into my work a decade later.

    Nature is by definition perfect and the embodiment of sacred geometry. Everything that has to do with composition and harmony can be found in nature. I approach my nature pieces like a giant bouquet, trying to find that perfect hidden balance between chaos and order. Paring down something as complex as plants, birds and trees is an incredible challenge but one that fills me with joy.

Nature

Garden Parties, *Ville de Lausanne*
Festival poster, 2018

Rice Fields, *Kuoni Travel*
Editorial illustration, 2017

Altiplano, *Kuoni Travel*
Editorial illustration, 2017

(Next Page)
Violeta, *Siempre Playa Project*
Promotional poster, 2018

Kitty, *Siempre Playa Project*
Promotional poster, 2018

Glenda, *Siempre Playa Project*
Promotional poster, 2018

(Next Page)
Bouquet, *Oé*
Wine label, 2021

103 Nature

La Jungle, *Warby Parker*
Mural illustration, 2019

(Next Page)
Birds of Paradise, *Bucherer*
Window display illustrations, 2021

Baboon
Personal work, 2018

Toucan
Personal work, 2018

Zebre, *Touchwood*
Exhibition illustration, 2019

(Next Page)
Peacocks & Flowers, *Heals*
Textile collaboration, 2015

Within any optical illusion lies a bit of magic. There is something very playful but also challenging in controlling what someone sees and how their brain interprets impossible shapes. Much like negative space, patterns provide the opportunity for some very powerful visual tricks.

My interest in patterns and in the Op Art movement in general began in art school where I discovered the likes of Bridget Riley, Victor Vasarely and Daniel Buren. I was fascinated by the effect their images had on my interpretation of reality. They made me feel strange, but in a way that was stimulating to the brain. I was particularly interested in optical illusions created by the repetition of lines and shapes.

The idea in most of my pattern-based work is to use figurative elements to interfere with the repetition. Whether using a figure as the hero of the composition or as a little touch, there is always a story to my patterns – a hidden narrative that guides the viewer and helps them decode the image and its meaning. Keeping a level of visual surprise and dizziness is what makes it fun and like any other illustration work, it is about composition, scale and harmony. For that reason, I tend to limit my palette even more in pattern-based illustration. The real challenge is to find that balance between what is pleasing to the eye and manageable to the brain.

Patterns

Tennis Court, *Monreal London*
Spring-Summer campaign, 2014

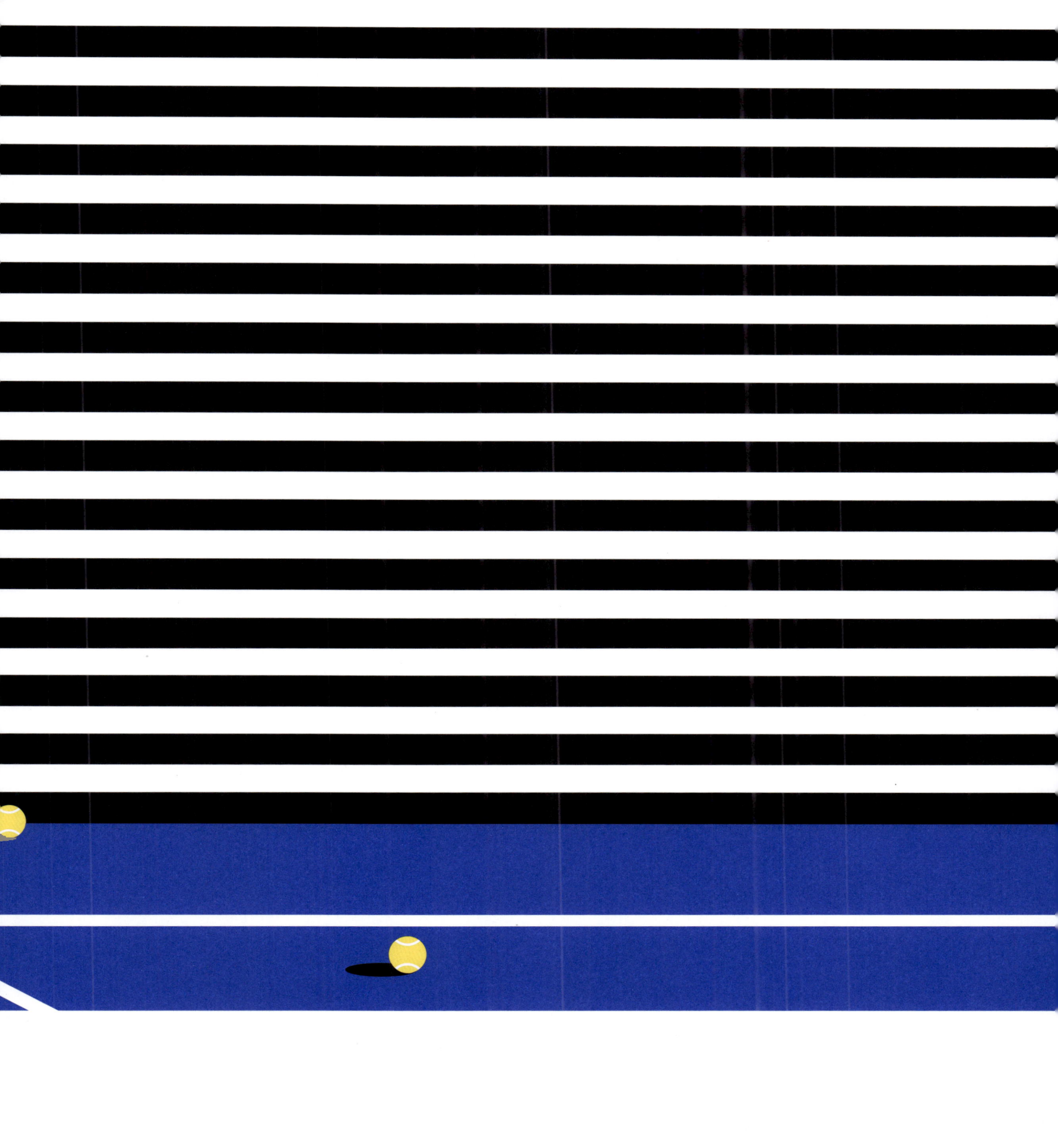

Alice, *Couronnes*
Textile collaboration, 2014

Misuzu
Private commission, 2015

Vera, *Marie-Claire*
Editorial cover, 2013

Suzie, *Aldo*
Spring-Summer campaign, 2013

Mother's Day, *Sephora*
Packaging, 2015

Bow Tie, *Sephora*
Window display, 2018

131 Patterns

The Leftovers, *The Washington Post*
Editorial cover, 2014

Seaside Gossip
Personal work, 2017

Balloons
Personal work, 2017

The Illustrator, *Gràffica*
Editorial Illustration, 2020

Terrain Vague, *Thomas Ollivier*
Wine label, 2017

(Next Page)
Paris Plages, *Ville de Paris*
Event poster, 2018

Blinds, *Hide&Seek Series*
Personal work, 2012

141 Patterns

Curtain, *Hide&Seek Series*
Personal work, 2012

Steps, *Hide&Seek Series*
Personal work, 2012

Balcony, *Hide&Seek Series*
Personal work, 2012

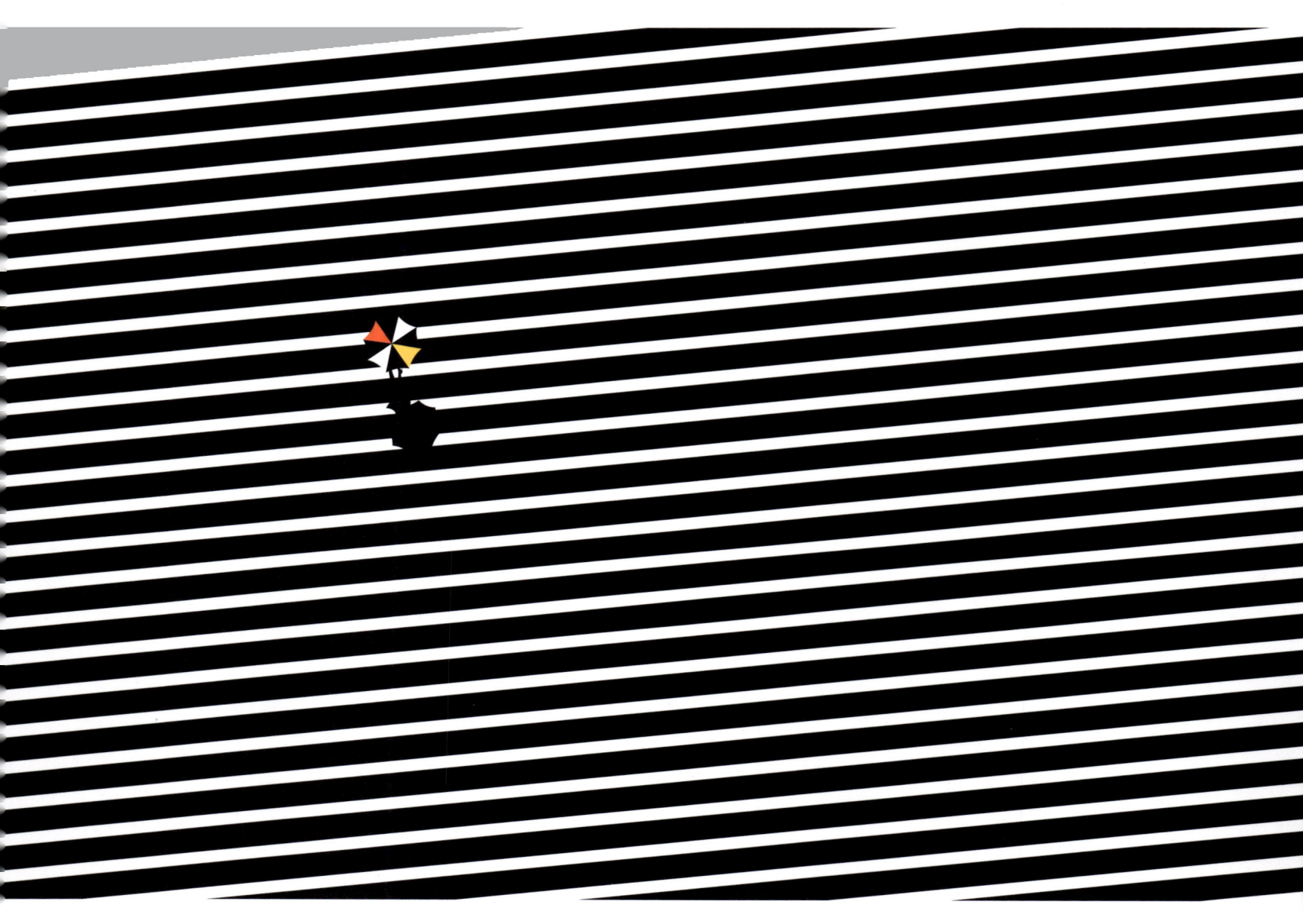

145 Patterns

Zebra, *Hide&Seek Series*
Personal work, 2012

Geometry is everywhere. Every single being, plant, object and even landscape can be deconstructed into basic forms. It's almost like an encrypted language that nature, as the ultimate designer, uses to build the world we live in. When it comes to art, from Egyptian hieroglyphics to the Bauhaus and from the Renaissance to Constructivism, people have used the same geometric principles to try and achieve the perfect composition. Geometry is, in essence, the search for perfection.

I loved mathematics as a teenager but never really considered how much of an impact it would have on my work until decades later. In the early days of my career, I started using geometry without being fully conscious of it when exploring patterns and more abstract pieces. As my understanding of perspective and light deepened, so did my love for geometry.

Today, I use grids and geometric structures when I want to establish a systematic relationship between the various elements of a piece, looking for the perfect structure to build on. Even though the underlying grid later disappears behind the final image, the fact that it's there draws you in… and keeps you there.

Geometry

New Horizons, *Brummell*
Editorial cover, 2014

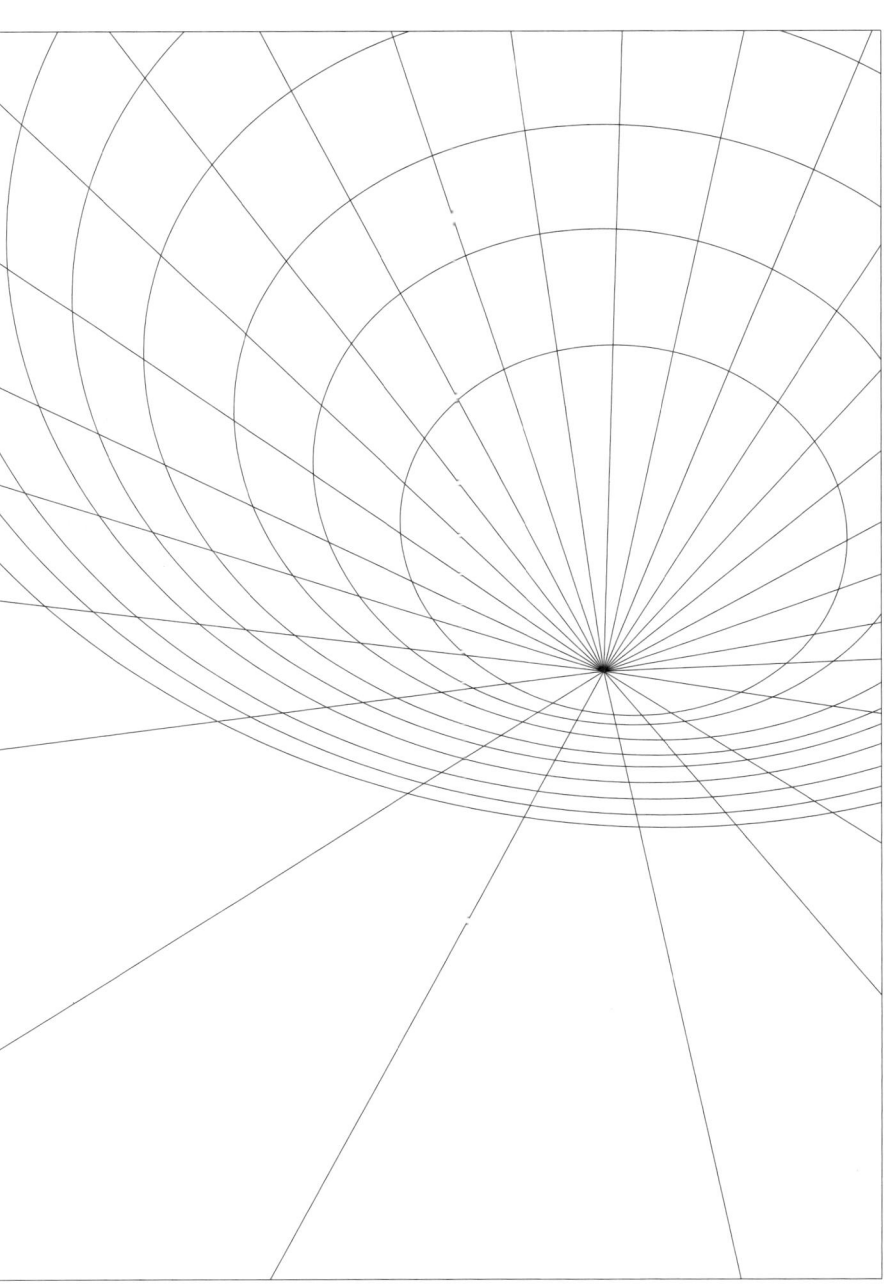

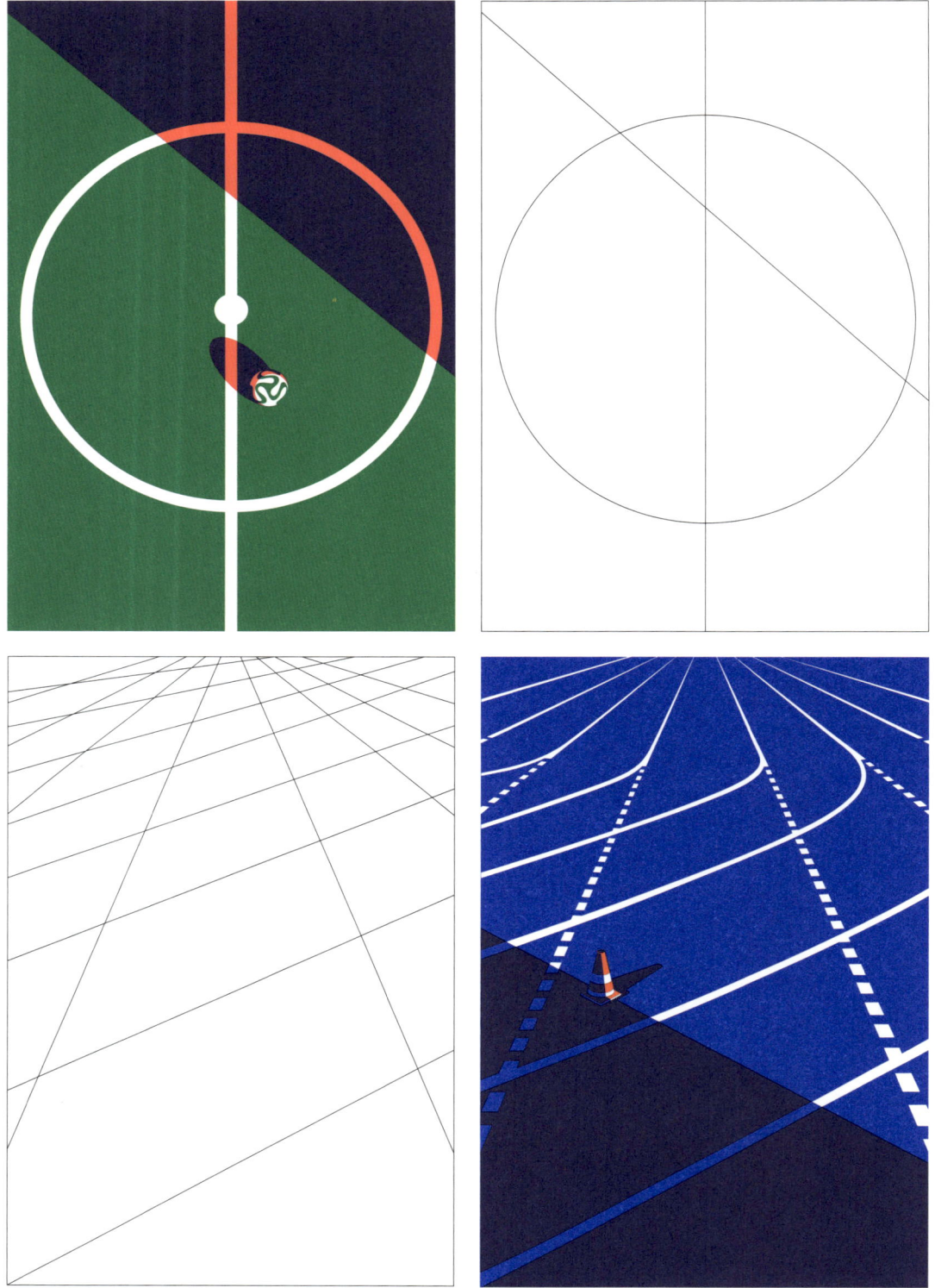

Midfield, *Sport&Style*
Editorial illustration, 2016

Track, *Sport&Style*
Editorial illustration, 2016

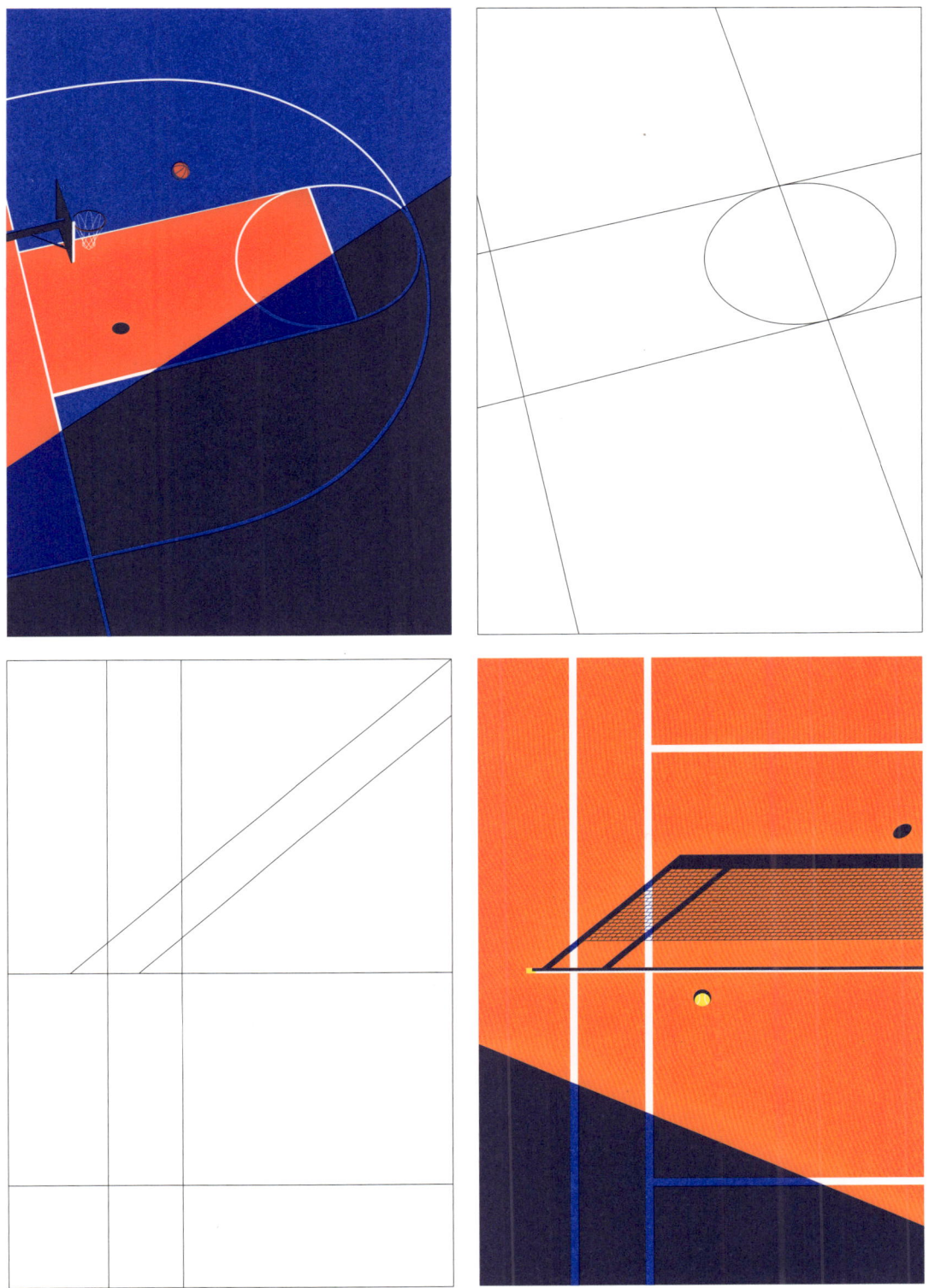

Hoop, *Sport&Style*
Editorial illustration, 2016

Match Point, *Sport&Style*
Editorial illustration, 2016

Geometry 152

Pool, *Sport&Style*
Editorial illustration, 2016

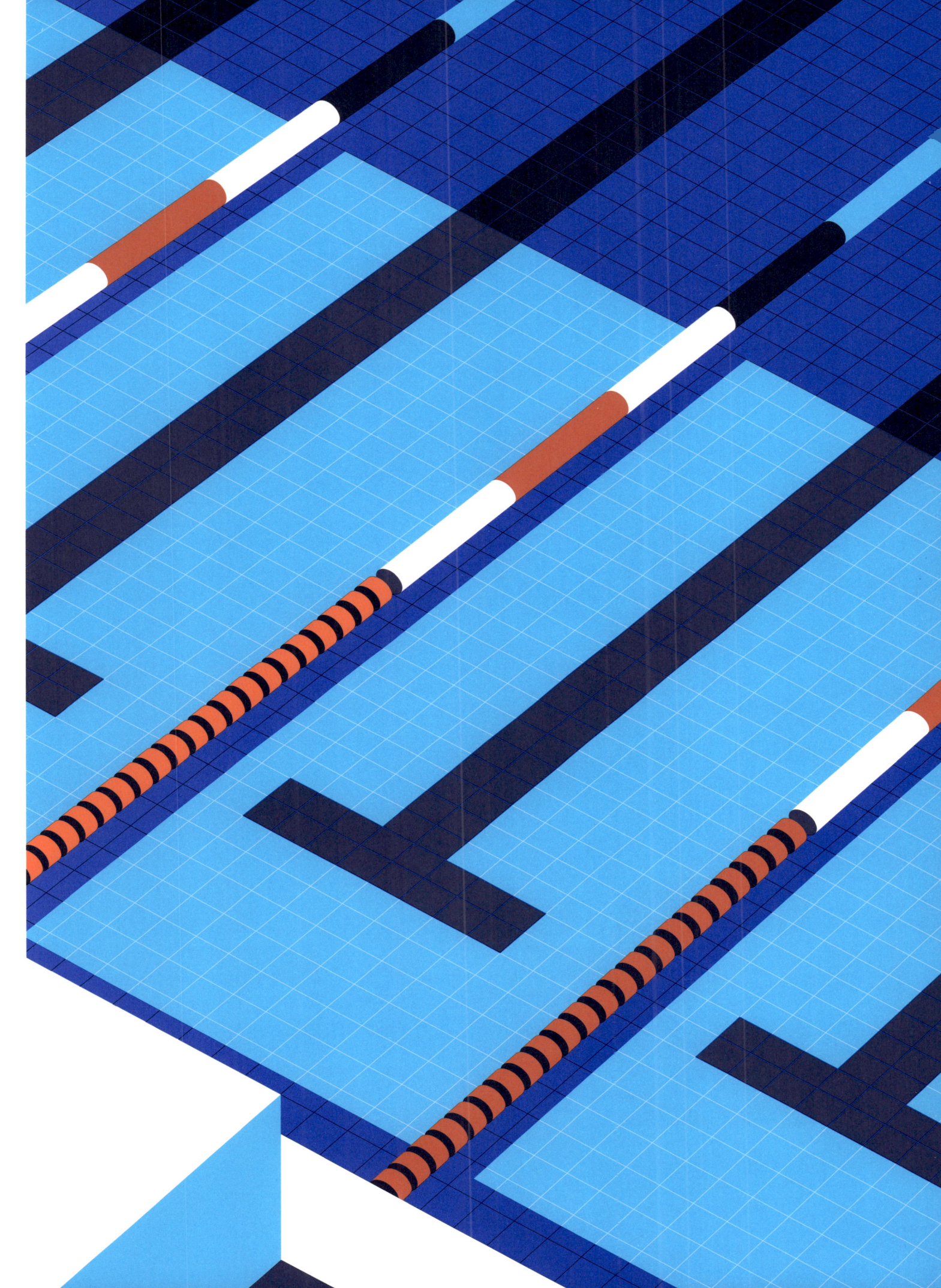

Travel Connoisseur, *Pullman*
Editorial series, 2013

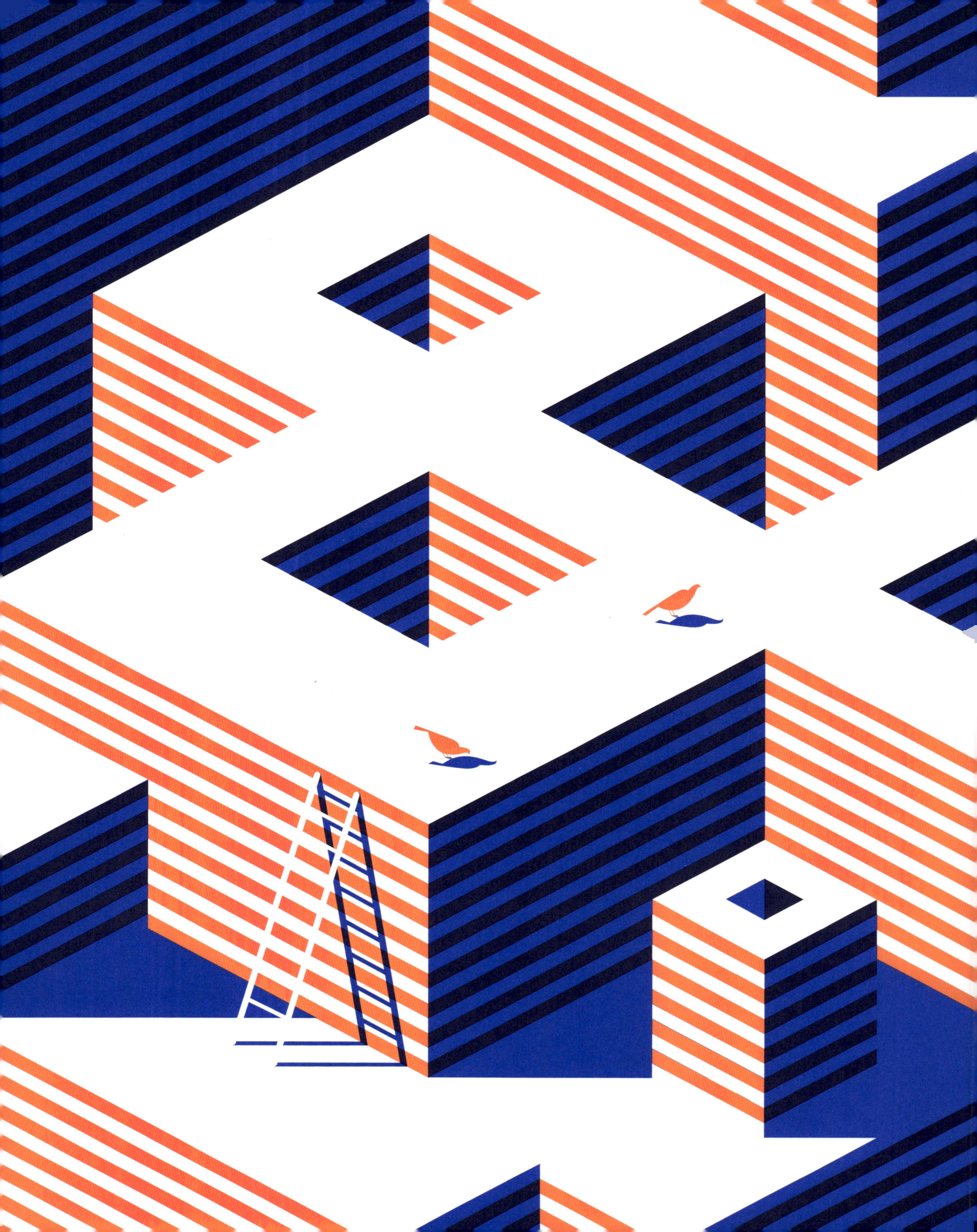

Ampersand, *The New Republic*
Editorial illustration, 2014

Rubik's Cube, *The Book of Everyone*
Editorial illustration, 2014

Kate, *Dark City Gallery*
Vertigo 60th anniversary poster, 2018

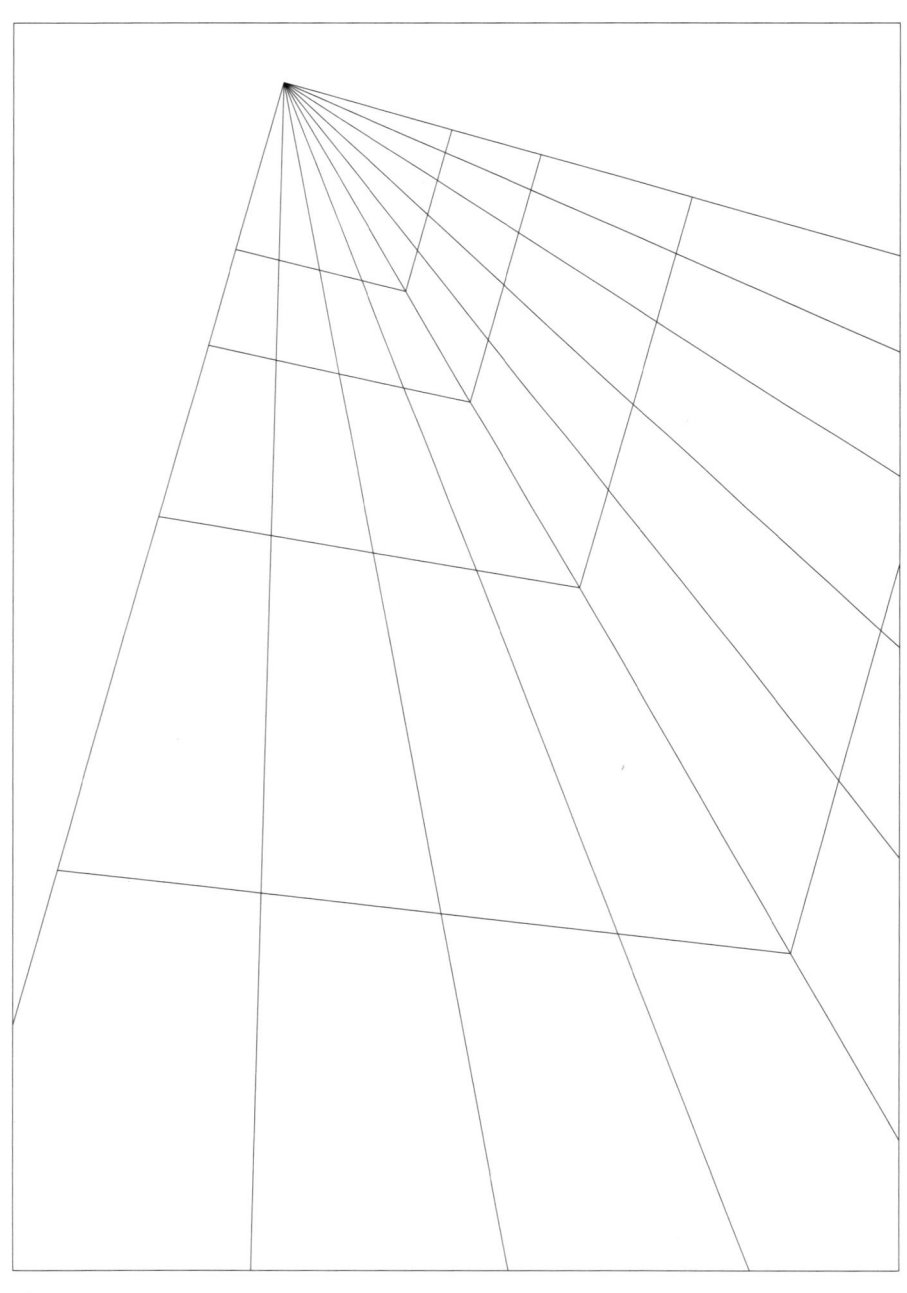

VERTIGO

A FILM BY **ALFRED HITCHCOCK**

JAMES STEWART KIM NOVAK BARBARA BEL GEDDES TOM HELMORE HENRY JONES
SCREENPLAY BY **ALEC COPPEL** AND **SAMUEL TAYLOR**   MUSIC BY **BERNARD HERRMANN**
BASED ON THE NOVEL D'ENTRE LES MORTS BY **PIERRE BOILEAU** AND **THOMAS NARCEJAC**

POSTER BY **MALIKA FAVRE** & **DARK CITY GALLERY**   VERTIGO © **ALFRED HITCHCOCK, LLC** ALL RIGHTS RESERVED

Geometry 160

James, *Dark City Gallery*
Vertigo 60th anniversary poster, 2018

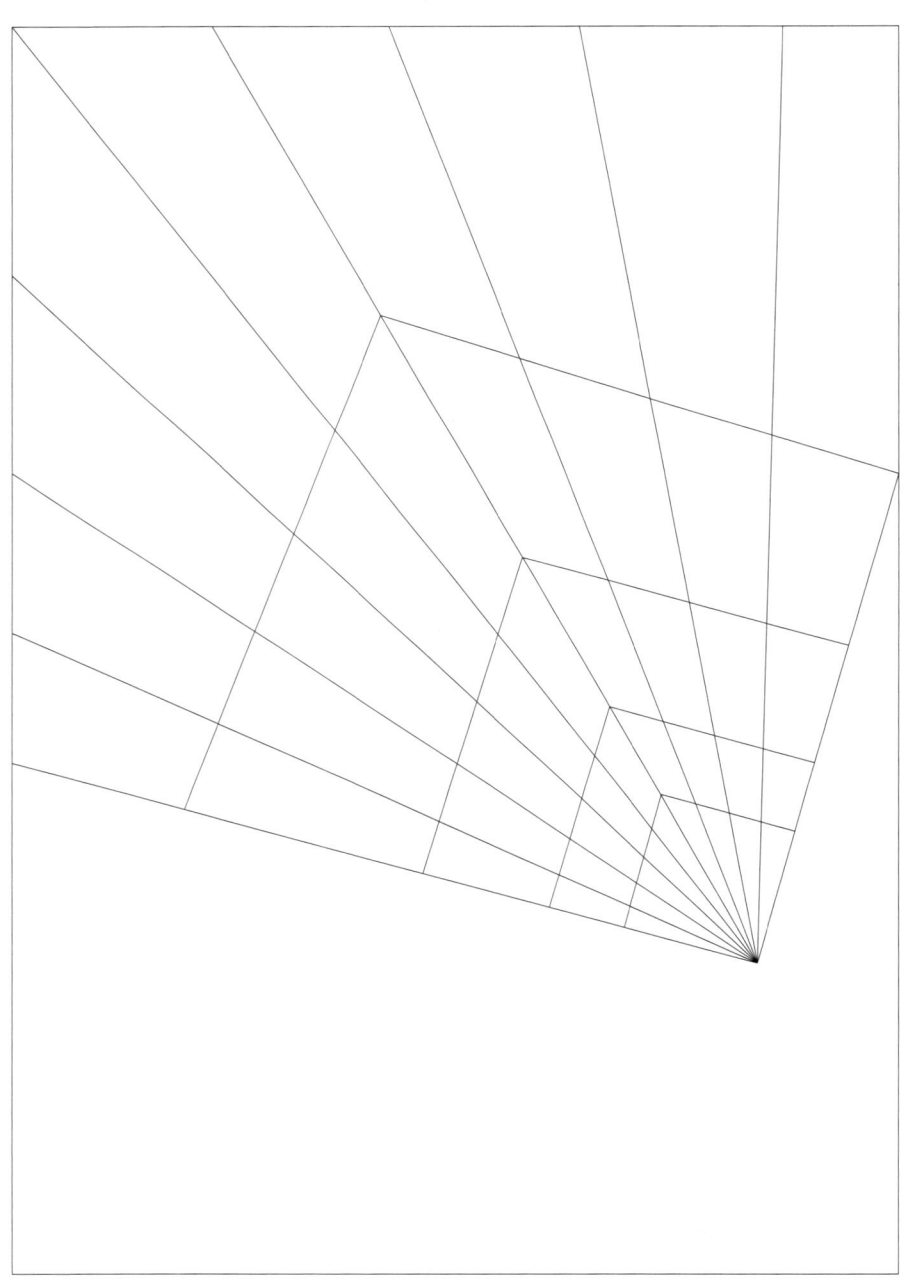

VERTIGO

A FILM BY **ALFRED HITCHCOCK**

JAMES STEWART KIM NOVAK BARBARA BEL GEDDES TOM HELMORE HENRY JONES
SCREENPLAY BY **ALEC COPPEL** AND **SAMUEL TAYLOR**   MUSIC BY **BERNARD HERRMANN**
BASED ON THE NOVEL D'ENTRE LES MORTS BY **PIERRE BOILEAU** AND **THOMAS NARCEJAC**

POSTER BY MALIKA FAVRE & DARK CITY GALLERY

VERTIGO © ALFRED HITCHCOCK, LLC ALL RIGHTS RESERVED

From Rotterdam with Love, *Metropolitan*
Editorial cover, 2018

Golden Ratio, *Graphic Design &*
Book contribution, 2014

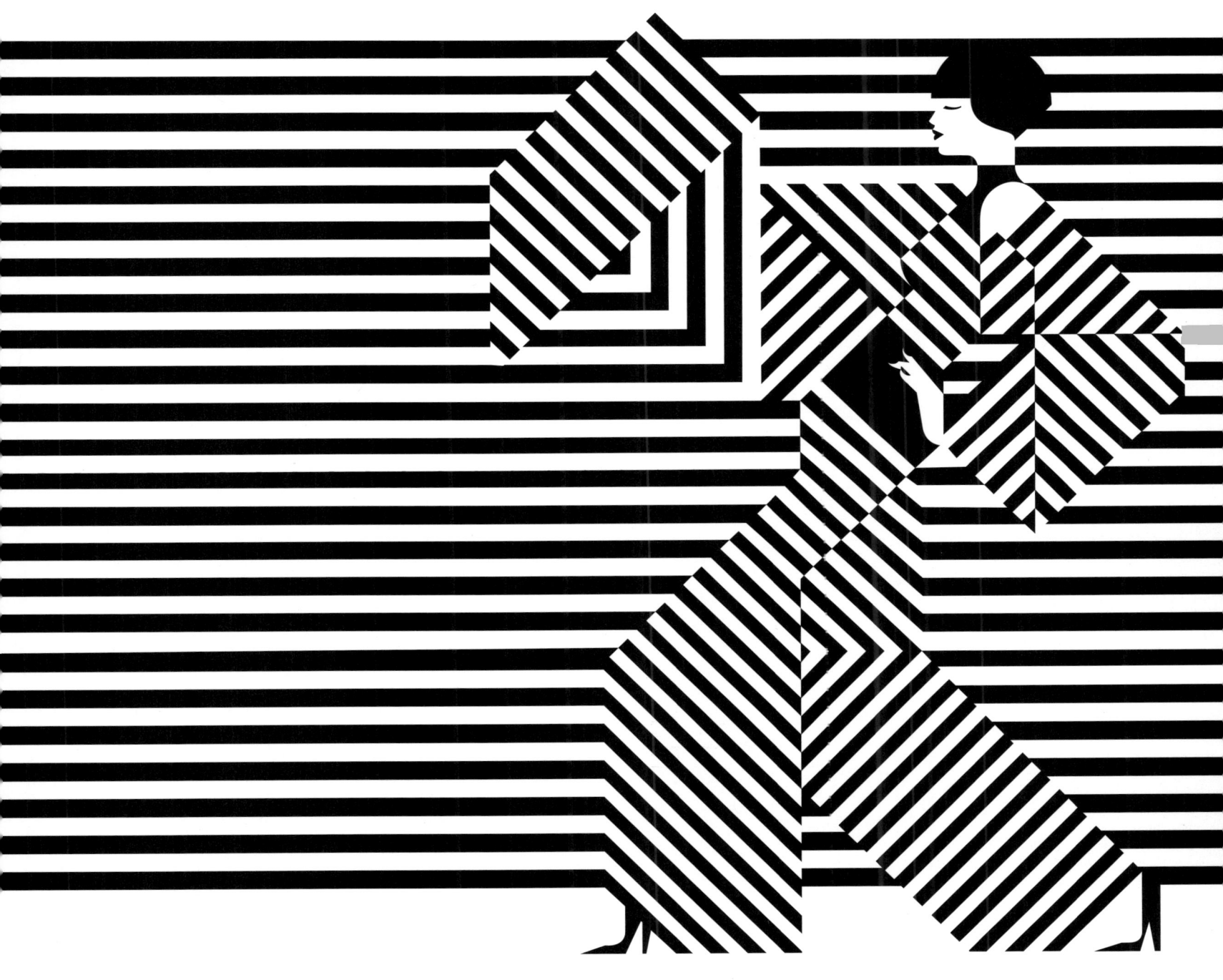

As a child, I wasn't really exposed to popular culture. I grew up in a household with no television and a pretty highbrow selection of music. Pop bands, TV shows and video games were basically banned but going to the cinema was a weekly occurrence. My parents would take my brother and I to see cartoons and new releases but also a lot of foreign films, 80s classics and black and white movies. My love of film began at that point and has never left me, influencing the way I compose and light my images. This cinematic approach to illustration – using unexpected angles and shadow play – led to my first commissions for the culture pages of *The New Yorker* as well as other movie-related projects.

My interest in pop culture, on the other hand, is something that developed later on. I've never been into pop icons or celebrity culture but I have embraced other things like social media, blockbuster movies, superheroes and other guilty pleasures I should probably keep to myself. On a visual level, I have always been fascinated by the powerful impact pop culture can have on all of us, and by how resonant its images can be. As an artist, I just love the idea of taking something that belongs to another time or place and reinterpreting it through the lens of today's visual culture. I also see it as a way to make my work accessible to everyone rather than the happy few.

Pop & Culture

The Grand Budapest Hotel, *BAFTA*
Program cover, 2015

Imitation Game, *BAFTA*
Program cover, 2015

Birdman, *BAFTA*
Program cover, 2015

Boyhood, *BAFTA*
Program cover, 2015

The Theory of Everything, *BAFTA* Program cover, 2015

The Big Reveal, *BAFTA*
Festival poster, 2015

Television Award, *BAFTA*
Program cover, 2015

Le Samourai, *The New Yorker*
Editorial illustration, 2017

Black Mirror, *The New Yorker*
Editorial illustration, 2016

Edna Buchanan, *The New Yorker*
Editorial illustration, 2015

Formation, *The New Yorker*
Editorial illustration, 2016

Vox Lux, *The New Yorker*
Editorial illustration, 2018

A Bigger Splash, *The New Yorker*
Editorial illustration, 2016

Paul McCartney, *The New Yorker*
Editorial illustration, 2020

Mostly Mozart, *Lincoln Center*
Festival poster, 2017

Viva Van Gogh, *Metropolitan*
Editorial cover, 2018

The Laureate, *The New Yorker*
Editorial cover, 2016

Behind the Lens, *The New Yorker*
Editorial cover, 2020

Halston, *The New Yorker*
Editorial illustration, 2021

Danseuses, *51th Montreux Jazz Festival*
Festival poster, 2017

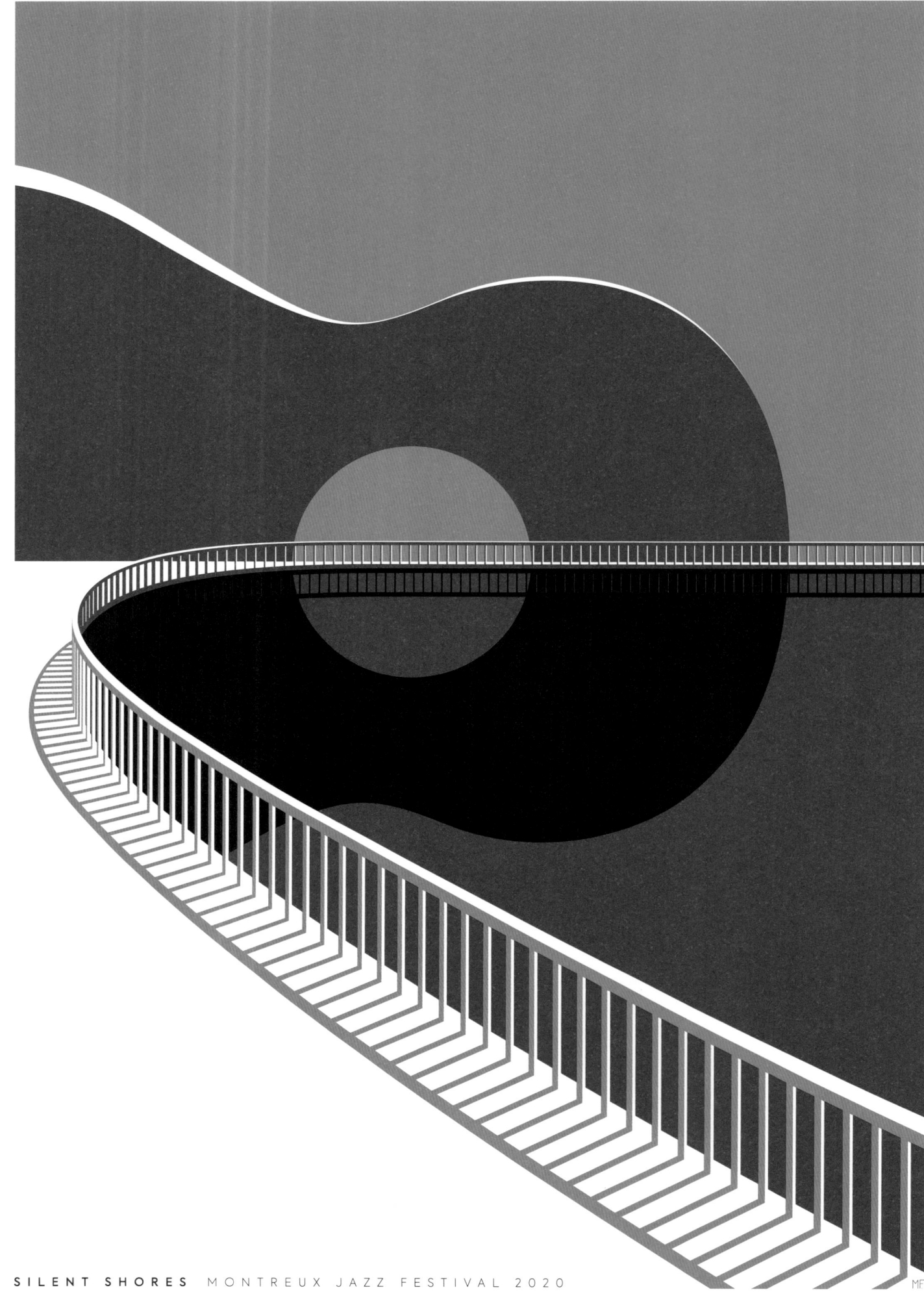

Silent Shores, *Montreux Jazz Festival*
Festival poster, 2020

Muhamed Ali, *Parkylife*
Personal work, 2020

Cabaret, *Little White Lies*
Alternative movie poster, 2012

Carrie, *Little White Lies*
Alternative movie poster, 2012

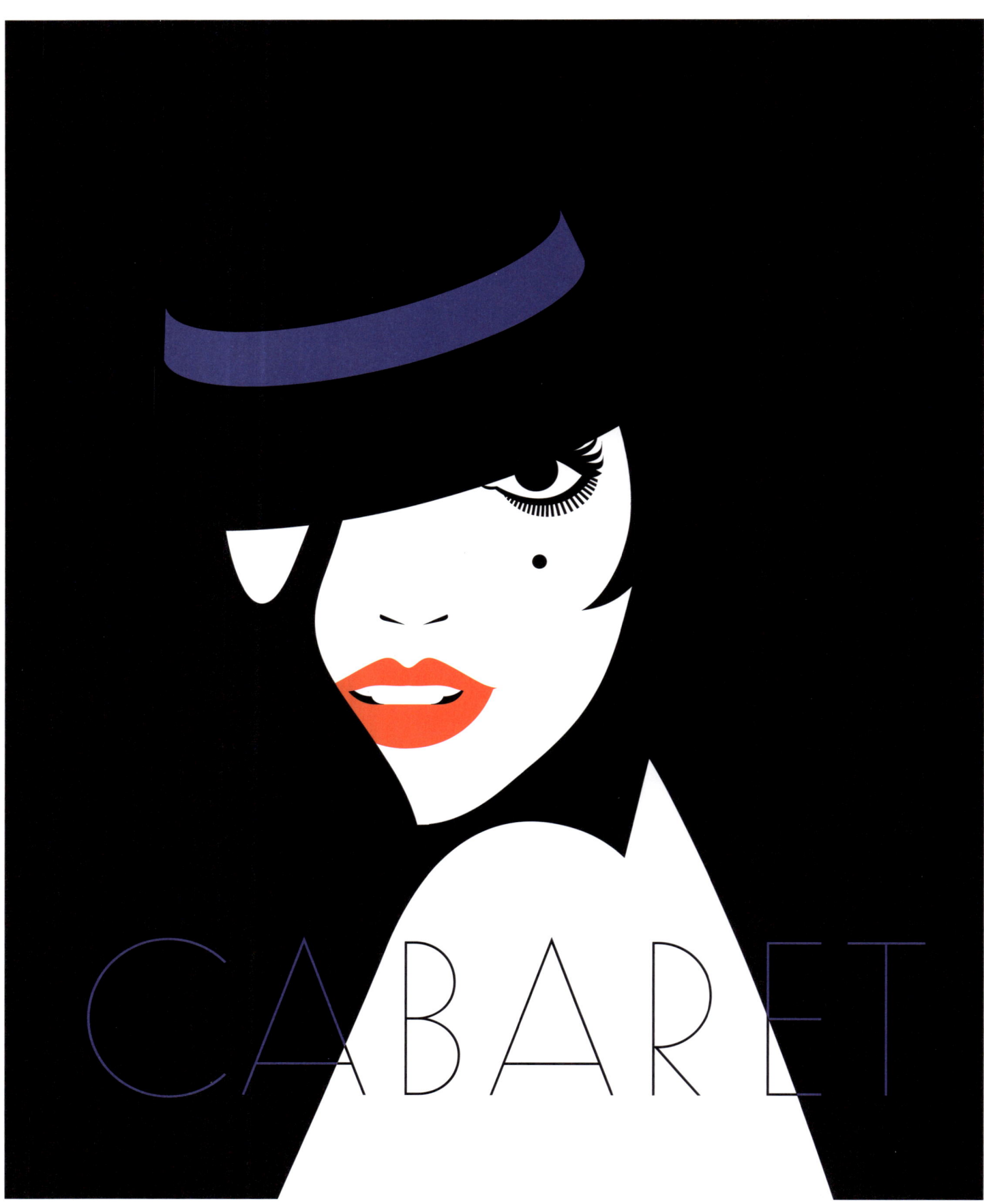

Romain Gavras, *Little White Lies*
Editorial illustration, 2012

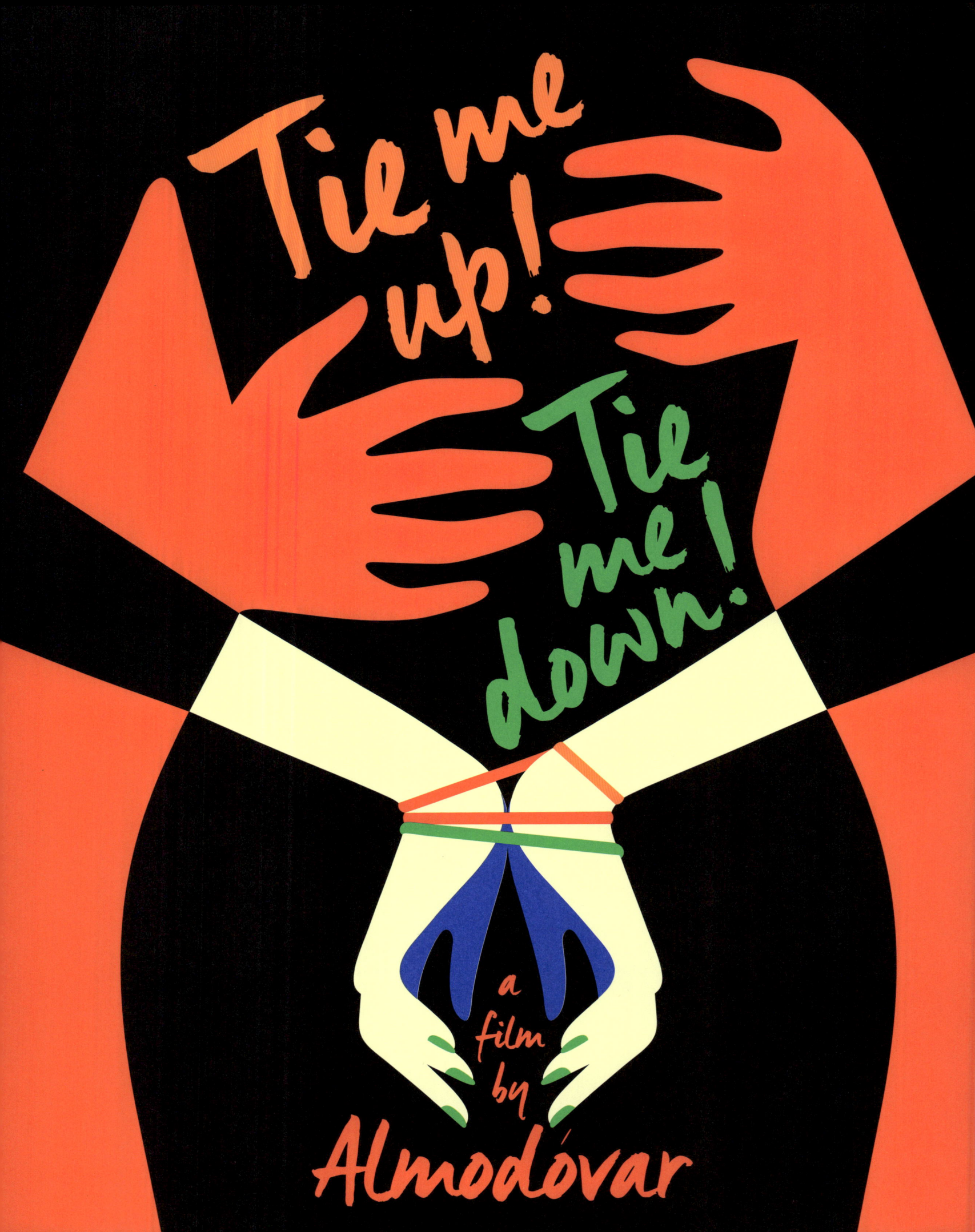

Tie me up! Tie me down!, *Criterion*
DVD cover, 2015

Women on the Verge of a Nervous Breakdown, *Criterion*
DVD cover, 2017

Typography by Tyrsa

Developed over the last few years, this body of work is my most recent. Prior to that, I didn't consider my work to be political or polemical in any way. Ironically, I am a very opinionated person but somehow I didn't really feel that this was the place to express it and as a consequence most of my career has focused on creating beautiful and strong imagery for people to enjoy, including myself. I was developing my craft, refining my style and growing as a person. Some might say that there was always something deeper, an invisible voice behind all the strong and powerful women I portrayed, and they might be right, but it wasn't something that I did consciously.

    The turning point came when I started working on *New Yorker* covers a couple of years back. The exercise was something I hadn't tackled before. It wasn't just about creating a striking cover, it was about being a mirror for society. The more covers I created, the more excited I felt about doing more of them. Little by little, cover by cover, my voice grew stronger. Seeing how an image based on personal experience can resonate with so many people out there and give them a voice too has been one of the best experiences of my career and pushed me out of my comfort zone. Not only did it change the way I select projects and approach illustration as a whole, it also really changed me as a person.

Society

Morality Plays, *Modus*
Editorial cover, 2016

St. Augustine and the Invention of Sex, *The New Yorker*
Editorial illustration, 2017

Start your Engines, *Arab News*
Editorial cover, 2018

The First, *The New Yorker*
Unpublished editorial cover, 2016

Operating Theatre, *The New Yorker*
Editorial cover, 2017

Coding 101, *The New Yorker*
Editorial cover, 2017

The Butterfly Effect, *The New Yorker*
Editorial cover, 2018

Joan Didion, *The New Yorker*
Editorial illustration, 2021

Fire Escape, *The New Yorker*
Editorial cover, 2020

On the front Line, *DAC*
Editorial illustration, 2020

Symphonie au Balcon, *Vogue Spain*
Editorial cover, 2020

Healthcare, *Geschichte*
Editorial Illustration, 2020

Populism, *Geschichte*
Editorial Illustration, 2020

The Truth is Out, *The Washington Post*
Editorial illustration, 2015

Park Avenue, *The New York Times*
Editorial illustration, 2015

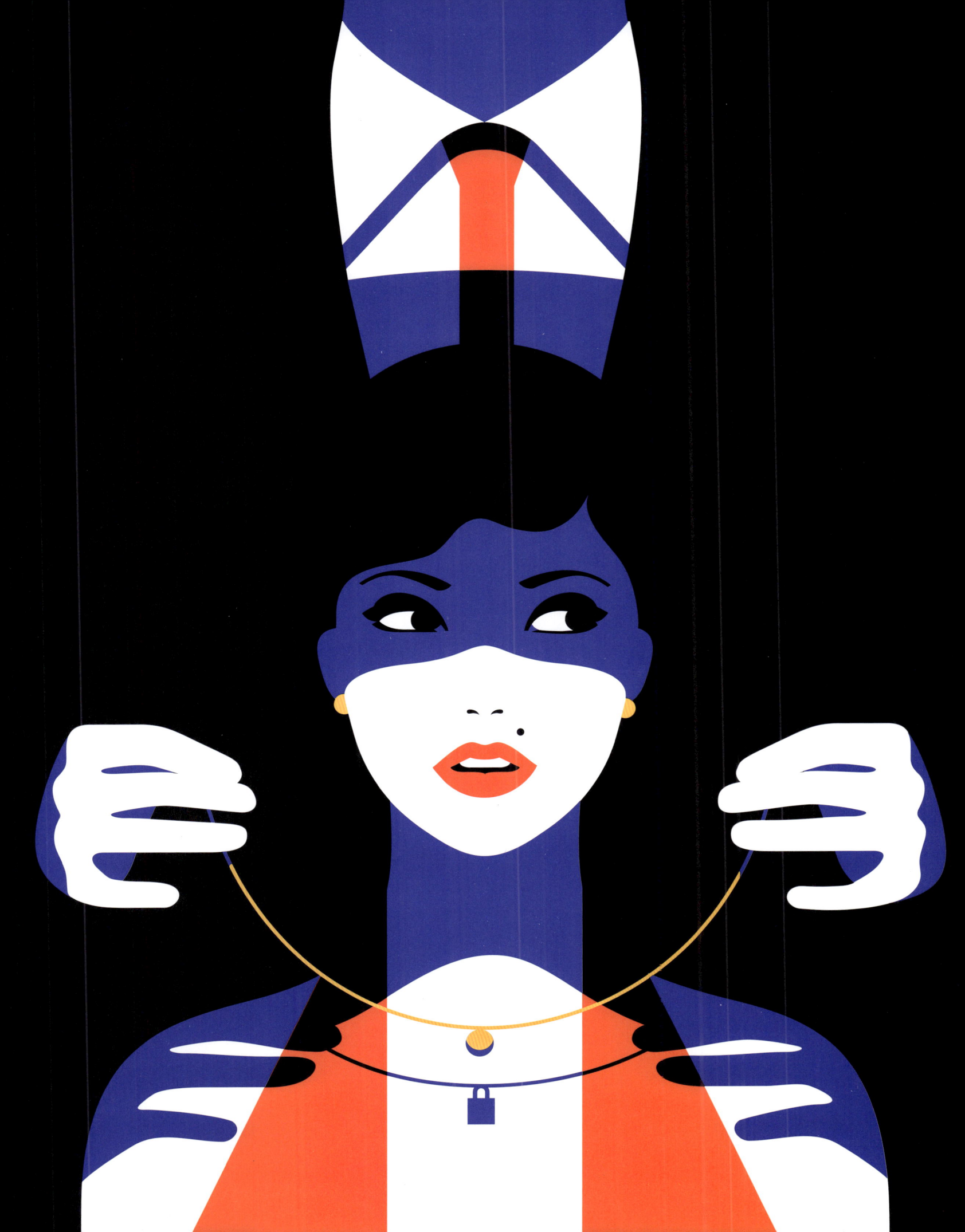

Women in Space, *National Geographic*
Editorial illustration, 2019

Colour & Light, *The New Yorker*
Editorial illustration, 2019

Reveal, *Where are the Boss Ladies*
Header illustration, 2018

Domestic Violence, *United Ways Canada*
Awareness campaign, 2018

Homelessness, *United Ways Canada*
Awareness campaign, 2018

225 Society

This Impossible Light, *Penguin Books*
Book cover, 2016

(Next Page)
Love(s), *Arrels Barcelona*
Textile pattern, 2018

La Fin du Rêve Américain, *Telerama*
Editorial cover, 2016

Women's Voices will be Heard, *Resist!*
Editorial cover, 2017

The Social Climber Guide, *Penguin Books*
Book cover, 2014

Engagées, *Webedia Books*
Illustration series, 2021

To explain the role erotica plays in my work I have to go back to my childhood drawings, and one in particular, which my mother has carefully put aside for posterity. I was nine when I proudly presented her with a drawing of a dominatrix holding a whip. I can't remember the drawing, why I drew it or where the inspiration came from, but it's fair to say it holds significance here. I was lucky to be brought up in a very open family, where taboos were non-existent and communication was key. It shaped me as a person but it also shaped the of type work I would later create. What began as a hobby soon became an obsession. From art school right through to my graphic design job at Airside in London, my sketchbooks were filled with erotic art. The difference was that after 25 years of drawing sensual women I became pretty good at it.

When I started my career as an illustrator, erotica was an important part of my body of work. My first erotic alphabets gave me great exposure and put me on the map as an illustrator. In these pieces I used negative space to suggest sensuality without ever fully revealing it. At this time, most of the other erotic art I could find was created by men. I felt it was important for me to share my vision, as a woman, of what was sexy – sensuality and cheekiness mixed with a touch of humour.

Erotica is a reoccurring theme throughout my entire career. I realised very early on that it was the one subject I wasn't ready to commercialise or compromise on, probably because the topic is so personal to me. As such, I will keep exploring it for my own pleasure, and hopefully yours.

Erotica

Ciseaux
Personal work, 2015

Kiss
Personal work, 2018

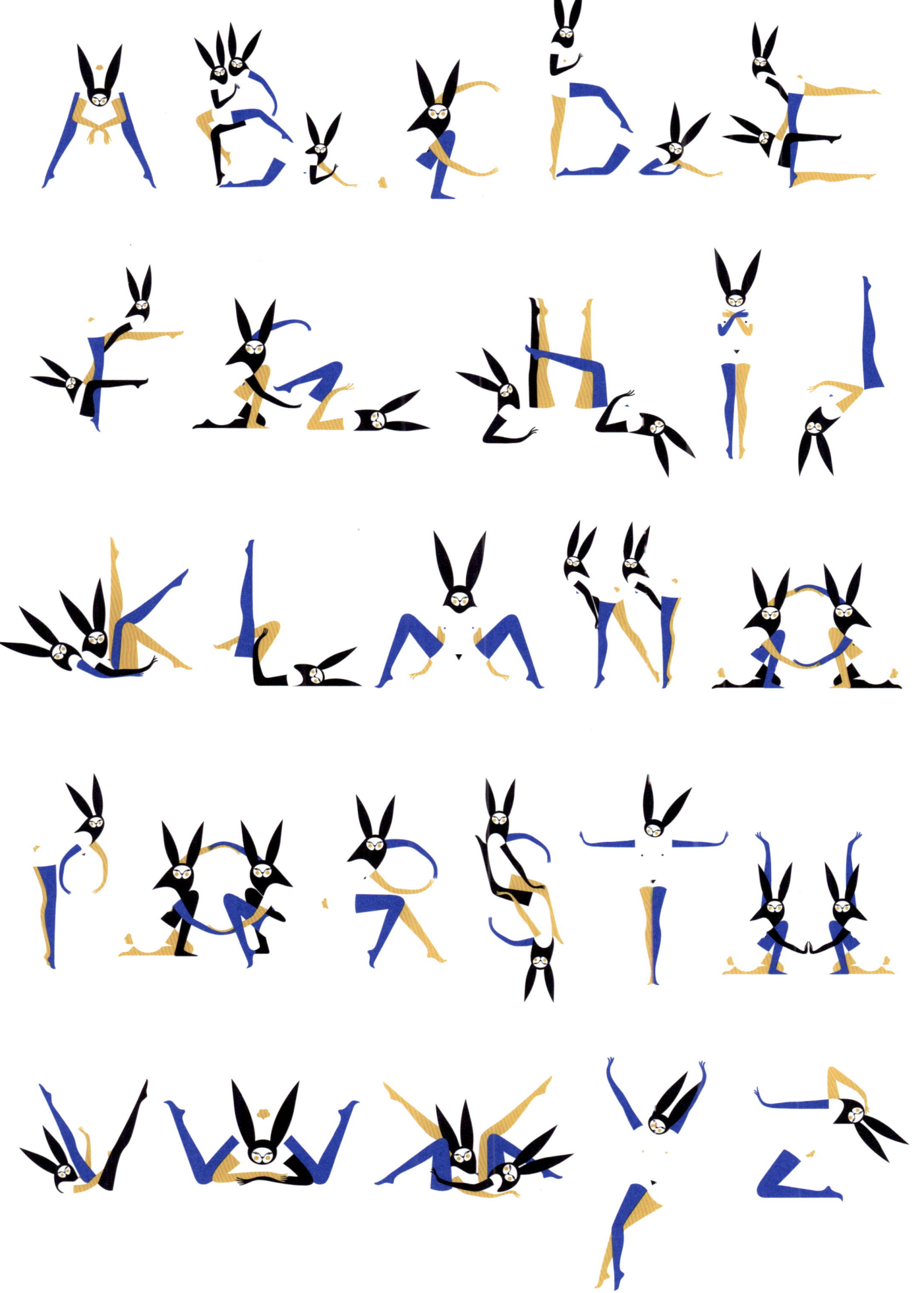

Persienne, *Crazy Horse Series*
Personal work, 2017

Respiration, *Crazy Horse Series*
Personal work, 2017

Apparition, *Crazy Horse Series*
Personal work, 2017

Demi-Lune, *Crazy Horse Series*
Personal work, 2017

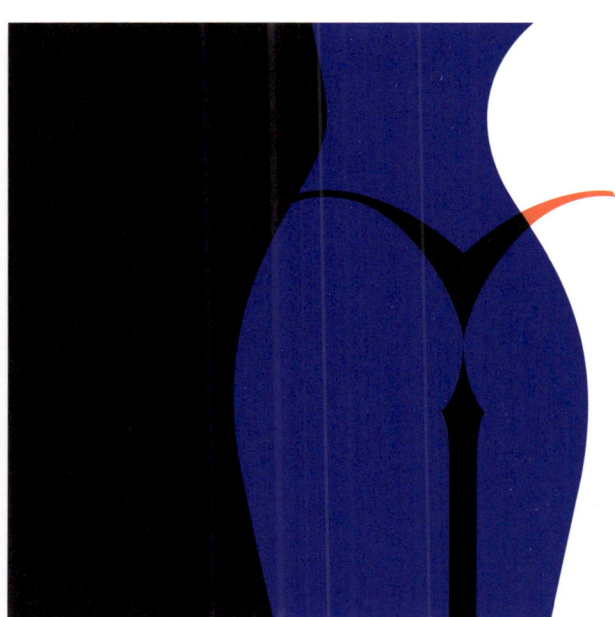

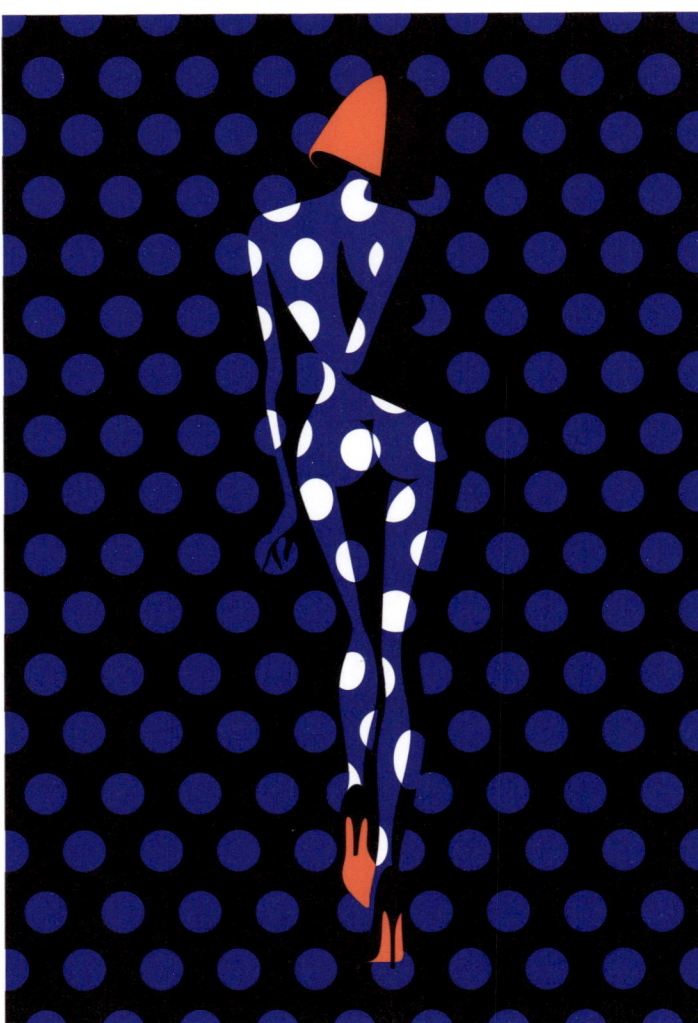

Le Zebre, *Crazy Horse Series*
Personal work, 2017

Polka, *Crazy Horse Series*
Personal work, 2017

Au pas, *Crazy Horse Series*
Personal work, 2017

245 Erotica

247 Erotica

Amuse-bouche, *Crazy Horse Series*
Personal work, 2017

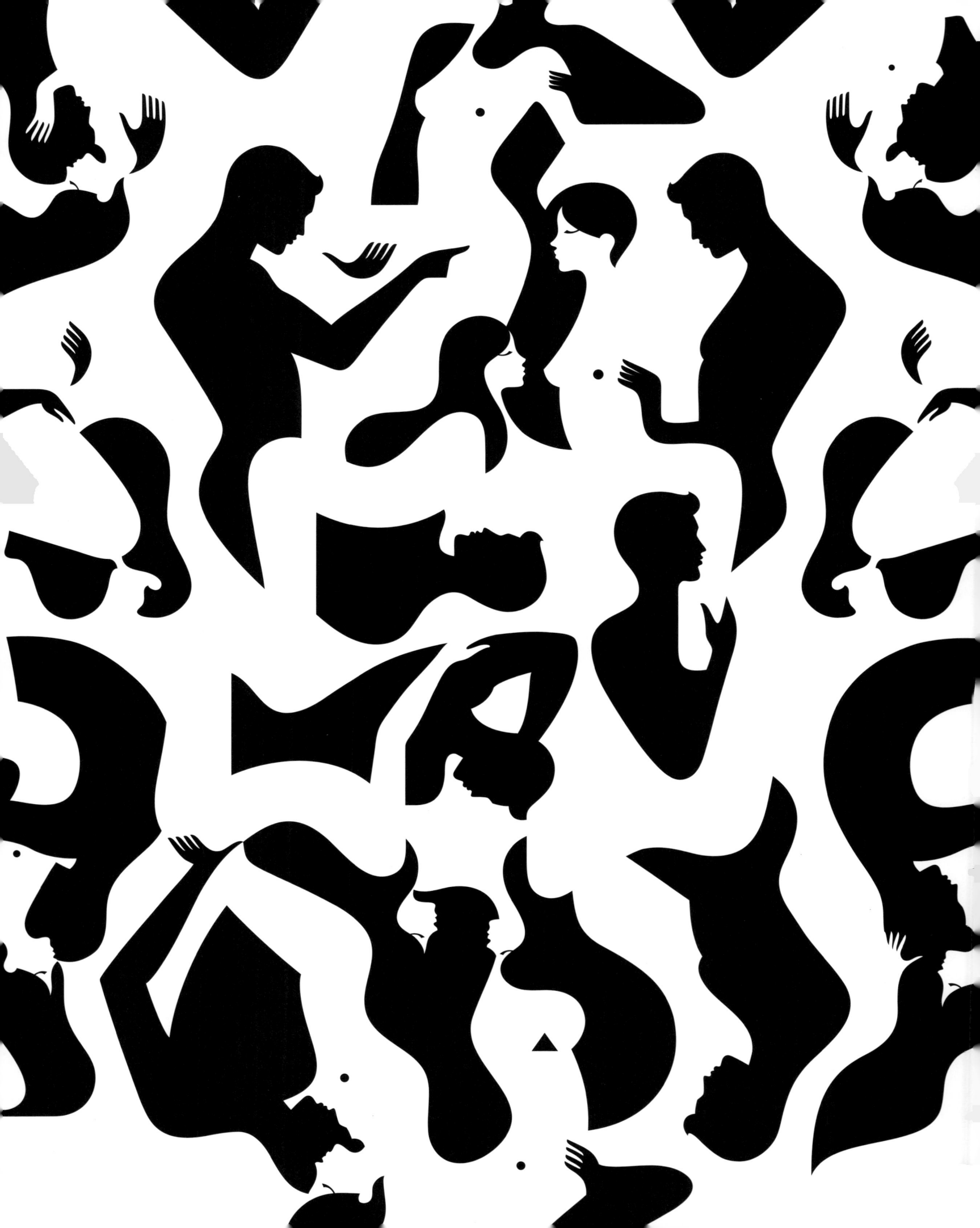

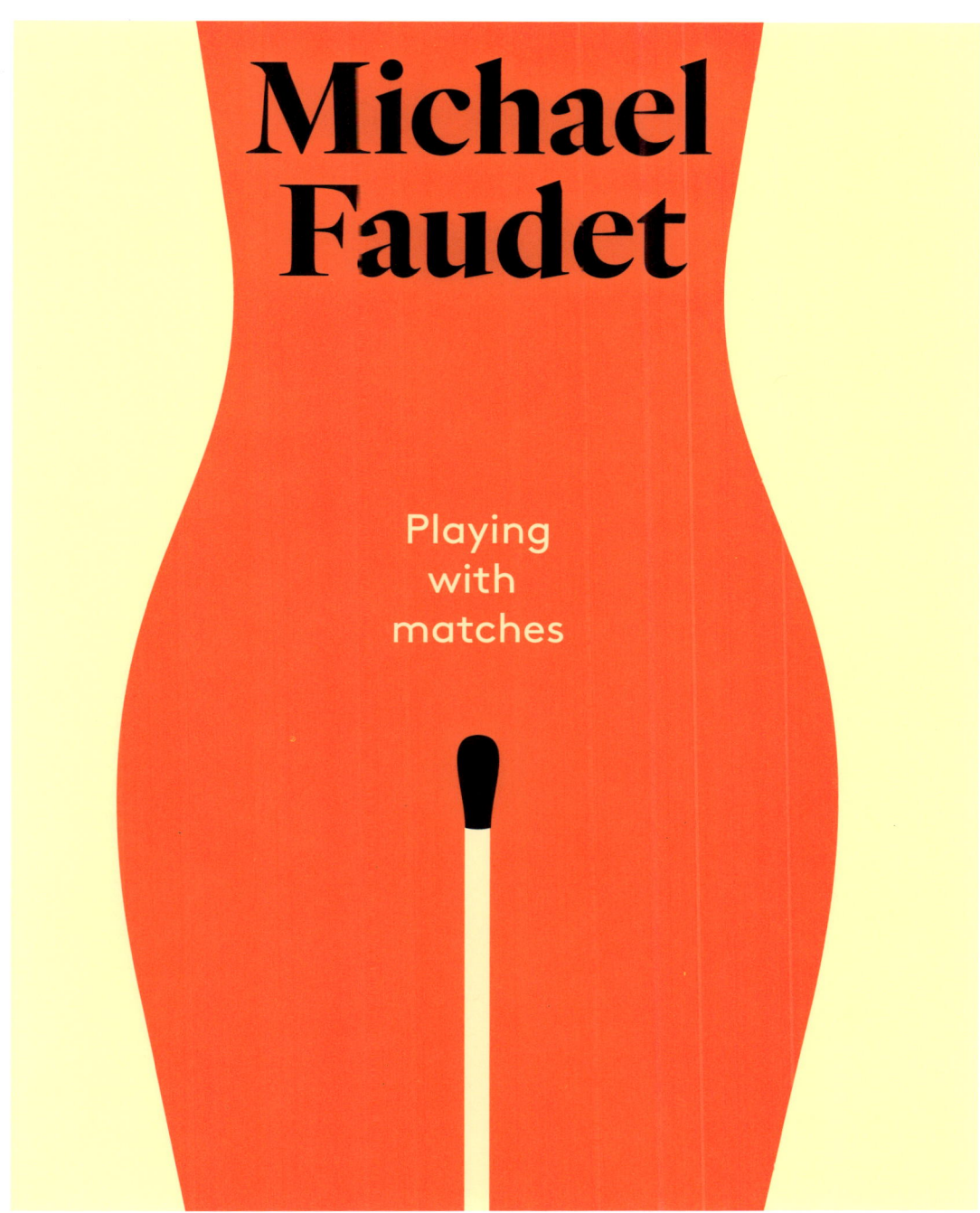

Orgy
Personal work, 2014

Playing with Matches, *Andrews McMeel*
Cover illustration, 2021

What Women Want, *New York Times*
Cover illustration, 2015

69
Personal work, 2012

Esquisses
Personal work, 2011

255 Erotica

Sous les Jupes des Filles, *Form Fifty Five*
Interactive header, 2013

A to Z, *The Kama Sutra Project*
Personal work, 2013

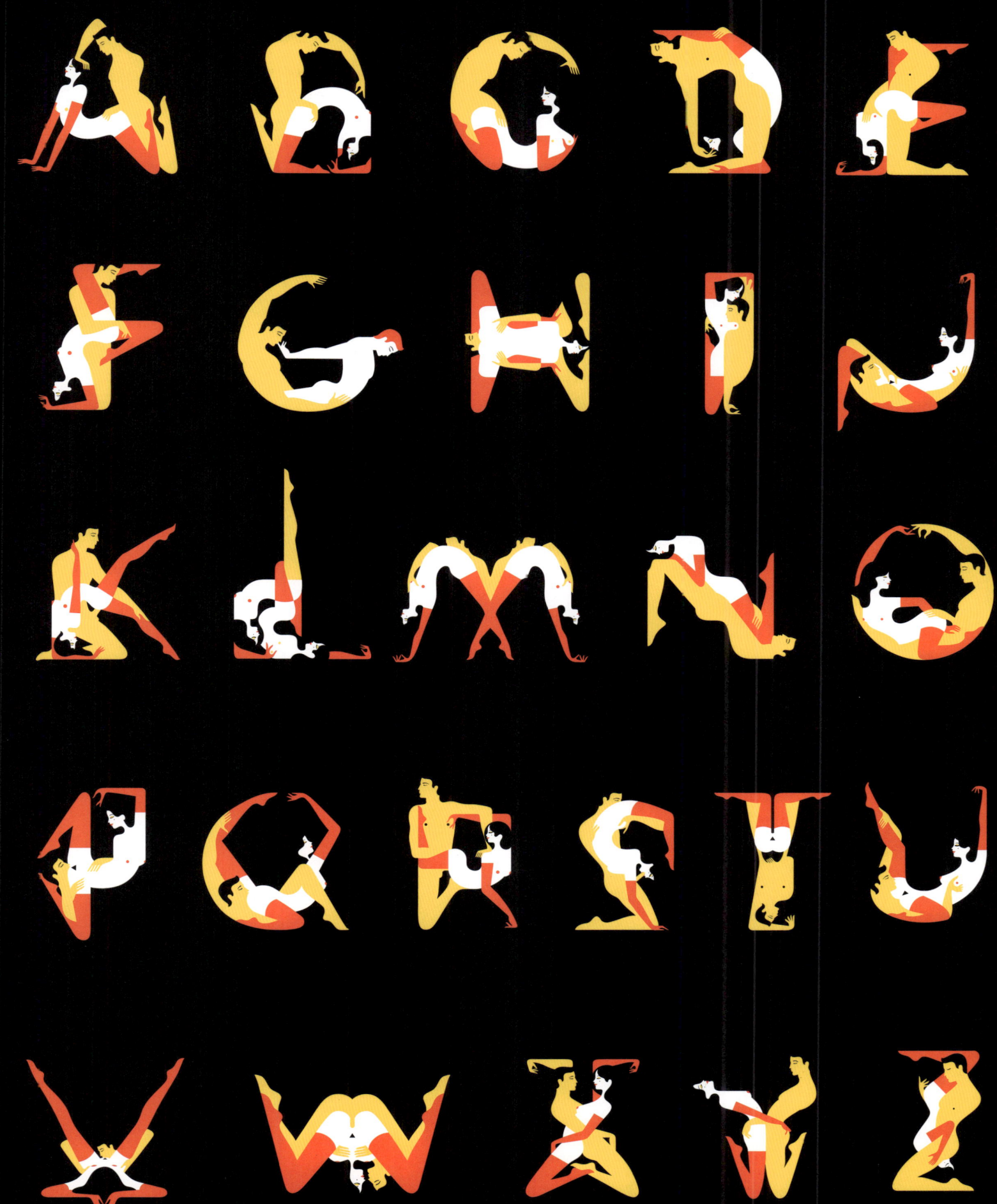

Erotica 262

263 Erotica

Acknowledgments

This first book marks an important moment in my journey as an artist. I want to start by thanking the two people who started it all, François and Ouiza. Without them, I wouldn't be here at all but more importantly without their openness, intelligence, and love, I wouldn't be the artist I am today. A very special thanks to my mum for teaching me how to draw, to my dad for teaching me how to be free, to my older brother and my whole family for their free-spirited eccentricity, inherited from Henri & Denise, the most unconventional and loving grandparents that ever lived.

To Jon and Tiphaine, my brilliant agents and to all the art directors who trusted me along the way, especially to Françoise and Genevieve who are a delight to work with.

To my little helpers, Dominika, Thomas and Lea for helping me keeping it together all these years and to all my friends, old and new for keeping me grounded.

To Garrick, for his deep understanding and thoughtful writing.

To Vladimir, my other half, for his love and all his precious help with this book.

And finally, to Céline & Jon, for making it happen.

Counter-Print
© 2022 Counter-Print
counter-print.co.uk
info@counter-print.co.uk

British Library cataloguing-in-publication data:
A catalogue of this book can be found in the British Library.

ISBN: 978-1-8381865-8-6

First published in the United Kingdom in 2019 by Counter-Print. Reprinted in 2020.

This revised and expanded edition printed in 2022.

Edited and produced by Counter-Print.

Design: Jon Dowling & Céline Leterme
Typefaces: Circular
Printing and Binding: Graphius, Belgium

Copyright on projects and their related imagery is held by Malika Favre.

Malika Favre
malikafavre.com
bonjour@malikafavre.com

All rights reserved. No part of this book may be reproduced, stored in a retrieval system, or transmitted in any form or by any means without prior written permission from the publisher.